HURRICANE HARVEY

DISASTER IN TEXAS AND BEYOND

Rebecca Felix

Ⅿ MILLBROOK PRESS / MINNEAPOLIS

A portion of the proceeds from this book will be donated to the Texas Library
Association's Disaster Relief Fund: http://www.txla.org/groups/DRC-funds.

Millbrook Press
A division of Lerner Publishing Group, Inc.
241 First Avenue North
Minneapolis, MN 55401 USA

Main body text set in Chaparral Pro 13/18
Typeface provided by Abode Systems

For reading levels and more information, look up this title at www.lernerbooks.com.

Library of Congress Cataloging-in-Publication Data

The Cataloging-in-Publication Data for *Hurricane Harvey* is on file at the Library of Congress.
ISBN 978-1-5415-2888-8 (lib. bdg.)
ISBN 978-1-5415-2889-5 (eb pdf)

Manufactured in the United States of America
1-44750-35700-11/6/2017

CONTENTS

A NASA satellite image shows massive Hurricane Harvey swirling over the Gulf Coast.

CHAPTER 1
ALMIGHTY STORM

In August 2017, one of the costliest weather disasters in US history hit Houston, Texas. Hurricane Harvey had winds that tore apart buildings and storm clouds that dropped trillions of gallons of rain. For days, the hurricane dumped rain on the city and surrounding areas. Soon, bayous overflowed and tributaries spilled over. Water from the vast San Jacinto River rushed across the county. Citizens watched as streets were submerged and cars sank. Houses were flooded, some with water up to their rooftops. There were thousands of emergencies and injuries. Eighty-two people were killed by the storm and its unbelievable flooding. Recovery from the damage and destruction was predicted to last for years.

The destructive force known as Hurricane Harvey began in the Atlantic Ocean as a tropical depression. The tropical depression's winds gained strength as it traveled west.

WHAT IS A HURRICANE?

A hurricane is a type of tropical cyclone. A tropical cyclone is a low, rotating storm that starts over warm ocean water. There are several types of tropical cyclones depending on the speed of the wind. A tropical cyclone with a wind speed of 38 miles (61 kilometers) per hour or less is a tropical depression. A tropical cyclone with a wind speed of 39 to 73 miles (63 to 117 km) per hour is a tropical storm. A tropical cyclone with a wind speed of 74 miles (119 km) per hour or higher is a hurricane.

Hurricanes are divided into five categories based on the Saffir-Simpson hurricane wind scale.

The scale was developed in the 1970s by US engineer Herbert Saffir and US meteorologist Robert Simpson. Each Category has its own wind speed range.

HURRICANE CATEGORY WIND SPEEDS

Category 1: 74 to 95 miles (119 to 153 km) per hour
Category 2: 96 to 110 miles (154 to 177 km) per hour
Category 3: 111 to 129 miles (178 to 208 km) per hour
Category 4: 130 to 156 miles (209 to 251 km) per hour
Category 5: 157 miles (252 km) per hour or higher

Hurricane Harvey's winds push seawater over barricades and across the road in Kemah, Texas.

It became a tropical storm. By August 17, the storm was big enough to require warnings. Scientists named it Tropical Storm Harvey and warned Caribbean islands in the storm's path. Harvey would bring heavy rain, strong winds, and possible surges of seawater ashore. It was certain to cause destruction to communities in its path.

However, the storm weakened as it moved farther west. It was no longer a tropical storm when it crossed Mexico's Yucatán Peninsula on August 22. But experts warned that Harvey could grow stronger when it hit water again. With the right factors, it could even become a hurricane. It wasn't long before this prediction was proven right.

HURRICANE HARVEY

Harvey reached the Gulf of Mexico on August 23. As predicted, the storm grew stronger once it was at sea again. Harvey hit a warm spot in the water that gave the storm energy. It met winds that gave it strength. By August 24, Harvey's winds blew at 100 miles (161 km) per hour. Tropical Storm Harvey had become Hurricane Harvey.

WHAT'S IN A NAME?

Once a tropical cyclone becomes a tropical storm, it is given a name. If it later becomes a hurricane, the hurricane will have the same name. The World Meteorological Organization assigns names alphabetically. They switch between male and female names. A name may be reused after six years. However, if a storm is very destructive, its name is retired and not used again. Experts believe there will never be another storm named Hurricane Harvey.

People in the southeastern United States watched weather reports as Harvey hurtled toward them. The hurricane sped toward the Texas Gulf Coast. Many people hurried to evacuate, but others stayed put. They prepared to face the storm.

Within a day, Hurricane Harvey grew more intense, becoming a Category 4 hurricane. Its winds measured 130 miles (209 km) per hour. Harvey hit Rockport, Texas, on the evening of August 25. It caused tremendous damage there before moving up the Texas coast.

Although its winds whipped at incredible speeds, the storm itself moved slowly. It sat over southeast Texas for several days, dumping great amounts of rain on the area. Waterways overflowed, flooding entire cities. Harris County, Texas, saw the worst of the flooding. The county is home to the city of Houston, the fourth-largest US city. In the Houston area, water covered streets and then cars and then the lower floors of buildings. People, pets, and wildlife were displaced, and chaos began.

Palm trees' trunks can bend. This helps them survive hurricane-force winds.

Damaged and destroyed homes in Rockport, Texas

CHAPTER 2

IMMEDIATE IMPACT

As Hurricane Harvey approached the Gulf Coast, citizens prepared for the worst. Many evacuated, including about half the ten thousand citizens of Rockport, Texas, where Harvey first made landfall. The other half of the town's citizens stayed to face the storm. Josh Morgerman was in Rockport when Harvey arrived. However, Morgerman isn't a Rockport resident. He's a storm chaser who traveled to Rockport to witness the intense storm up close. He got his wish.

Hurricane Harvey's eyewall passed over Rockport during landfall. The eyewall is the storm's core, where its winds are strongest. Harvey's eyewall winds spun in many directions. "That's especially scary because debris is blowing every which way and if debris hits you at that speed, it's instant death," said Morgerman. He survived the winds, but at least one Rockport citizen died. Several others were injured.

Much of the city was badly damaged. Harvey's winds stripped leaves from branches and sent trees toppling to the ground. The trees landed on buildings and blocked roads. Signs, stoplights, and even large power lines snapped in two from Harvey's winds. The storm ripped roofs from buildings, broke windows, and crumbled walls. Some buildings completely collapsed.

Fallen trees and power lines surround a car submerged in floodwaters in Rockport, Texas.

HARVEY'S PATH

TEXAS

HOUSTON

7 LOUISIANA

6

5

MEXICO

GULF OF MEXICO

4

3

2

ATLANTIC OCEAN

1

1 August 17: Tropical Storm Harvey forms in the Atlantic Ocean.

2 August 22: Harvey weakens as it crosses the Yucatán Peninsula.

3 August 23: After reaching the Gulf of Mexico, it strengthens back into Tropical Storm Harvey.

4 August 24: Tropical Storm Harvey becomes Hurricane Harvey.

5 August 25: Harvey hits Rockport, Texas. It moves up the Texas coast to Port Lavaca.

6 August 26–27: Harvey moves to the Gulf of Mexico near the coast of Harris County. Its rain and damaging winds batter Harris County for four days.

7 August 30: Harvey makes its final landfall near Cameron, Louisiana.

"We've been devastated," said Rockport mayor C. J. Wax. "I have some buildings that are lying on the street."

SLOW-MOVING STORM

Harvey's eyewall passed over Rockport a second time on its way out of town. Its winds still spun at incredible speeds, but the storm itself crept up the Texas coast at only about

10 miles (16 km) per hour. In Port Lavaca, Harvey caused a massive storm surge to wash over the town. A storm surge is a flood of seawater that is pushed onto shore by the storm's wind. Water levels rose more than 6 feet (1.8 meters) in Port Lavaca. Seawater rushed through doors and windows. It swept cars from roads and carried boats ashore. Many boats that remained docked crashed against one another and sank.

Harvey left Port Lavaca, moving farther up the coast and inland. The hurricane was headed toward Harris County. County residents prepared for its arrival. Many nailed thin sheets of wood over the windows and doors of their homes and businesses. This was to keep glass in these entryways from breaking. People lined doorways with sandbags, which can keep water from entering a building.

With their properties as secure as possible, many residents left Harris County. The media shared images of the damage Harvey had done so far along the coast. Meteorologists warned people of the coming danger. But some people were not able to leave Harris County on their own. This included hospital patients, nursing home residents, and some disabled people.

Other county residents stayed because they had nowhere else to go. Some did not have vehicles or the money to pay for transportation. Still other Harris County residents stayed because they heard confusing advice. Some county leaders told people to leave. But other leaders told people to stay put. These leaders said people would be safer indoors than on the area's roads. Whether at home or on the road, the people of Harris County waited anxiously for Harvey to hit.

After boarding up windows and doors for protection against Harvey's elements, many people added messages begging the storm for mercy.

Harvey's floodwaters were so deep in places that the water nearly covered street signs.

CHAPTER 3
HITTING HARRIS COUNTY

Hurricane Harvey weakened as it moved inland, becoming a tropical storm again.
But it was still a very powerful storm with winds of up to 70 miles (113 km) per hour.
Harvey neared Harris County late on August 26. It created immediate damage, tearing
walls and roofs from buildings and homes, bending signs and toppling trees. Debris flew
across neighborhoods.

**Damage from a tornado caused by Harvey in
Missouri City, Texas**

But this damage wasn't caused only
by the storm's winds. When tropical
cyclones arrive on land, they can create
tornadoes. Like hurricanes, tornadoes
can destroy buildings and lift and carry
vehicles across entire cities.

More than one hundred tornado
warnings were issued in the Houston
area. At least sixteen tornadoes were
confirmed, with people taking videos
and photos of them. The threat of more
tornadoes remained. This was because
Harvey hung over Harris County for
days. As it did, wind and tornadoes
weren't the only concerns. People also
worried about the rain.

An aerial view of flooding in Houston, Texas

EXTREME FLOODING

Harris County residents worried about the rain for good reason, especially in Houston. The city of Houston is prone to flooding. It is very flat and is not very high above sea level. Houston is also large and urban. Much of its land is covered by roads, sidewalks, parking lots, and driveways. These hard surfaces do not soak up water the way soil does. This means rainwater has fewer places to drain. This can easily lead to flooding.

Flooded roads made travel extremely difficult. Marines used huge trucks to bring supplies to those who couldn't evacuate.

The large number of waterways in Houston is another factor making it likely to flood. There are several bayous, creeks, and tributaries near and in the city, and the San Jacinto River runs through the area as well. Harvey's rains caused these waterways to overflow. Experts believe Harvey dropped about 1 trillion gallons (3.8 trillion liters) of water on the area over four days. Nineteen areas around Houston received more than 40 inches (102 centimeters) of rain!

When the waterways overflowed, water rushed across streets and covered highways. It rose to car and truck doors. It leaked through doorways and into homes and businesses. As the rain continued, water levels rose further. Soon, about 70 percent of the county was under 1.5 feet (0.5 m) of water. As the rain continued, water levels rose even more. Vehicles were completely underwater. Water entered home and building windows, filling entire levels. Some homes had water up to their roofs.

Border Patrol agents used boats to rescue stranded residents. Thousands of members of government agencies helped in the aftermath of Hurricane Harvey.

CHAPTER 4
WATER RESCUES

Harvey's floodwaters forced tens of thousands of people from their homes. Thousands more were trapped in flooded houses, buildings, and cars. Between August 27 and August 30, more than three thousand requests for rescue were made in the Houston area.

Police officers and emergency responders sprang into action. They set out on boats to rescue as many people as possible. The US military sent emergency workers from other states to help. However, rescuers were still overwhelmed. There were just not enough of them to reach everyone in need. City leaders asked locals who owned boats to come to the aid of their neighbors.

CITIZEN HEROES

Unofficial rescue groups immediately formed across Harris County. These rescuers traveled flooded streets in kayaks, fishing boats, and anything that floated. Thirteen-year-old Virgil Smith used an air mattress. Virgil lived in Dickinson, a city outside Houston. Virgil and his mom's first-floor apartment flooded. An upstairs neighbor gave them shelter. Then Virgil's mobile phone rang. His friend's family was trapped in a building nearby. None of the family members knew how to swim.

A member of the Texas Army National Guard rescues a baby trapped by Harvey floodwaters.

WHAT DO ZOOS DO DURING HURRICANES?

Zoos do not free the animals during a hurricane. Many animals living in a zoo have never lived in the wild. They rely on zoo staff for food and shelter. Allowing these animals to run loose during a hurricane would be dangerous for the animals and the public.

Instead, zookeepers try to move the animals to safety within the zoo. This can create unusual situations. In 1992, Miami MetroZoo (now Zoo Miami) in Florida moved its flamingoes into a zoo bathroom during Hurricane Andrew. The bathroom's cement walls provided protection. The Houston Zoo didn't move any animals into bathrooms during Harvey. But several zoo employees stayed at the zoo to care for the animals.

Virgil swam over with his air mattress and rescued the family of five children and two adults. He went on to save twelve more people. Virgil swam back and forth, pushing people to safety on his air mattress.

Similar stories of citizens acting heroically were told around Harris County. People wading, swimming, or traveling by boat stopped to help others in need. They brought people to shelters and shared food, drinking water, and dry clothing.

Social media helped rescuers find flood victims. Many social media apps allow users to connect with users nearby, even if they are strangers. Some have ways for users to share their locations with one another. Thousands of rescues were made using these types of communication.

People also used social media to ask rescuers to help others. They posted photos of people stuck on roofs of flooded homes and alerted rescuers to people in need of help but without a way to communicate. This allowed rescuers to save many people they might not have otherwise known about. But these people weren't the only victims who weren't able ask for help. Harvey also left thousands of animals in need of rescue.

Thousands of pets were rescued and sent all around the United States to rescues or foster homes.

WHAT ABOUT THE ANIMALS?

Austin Hellweg, 129th Rescue Squadron special missions aviator, rescued a family's dog and helped move the family to safety after Hurricane Harvey.

During Hurricane Harvey, thousands of animals were lost, hurt, or put in danger. Many people took their pets with them when they evacuated. Others carried or swam their animals to safety during the storm. One Houston pet owner made her small dog a boat out of a bucket!

But many people were separated from their pets. Some pets ran away or were trapped during flooding. Others were left behind when their owners got hurt or were rescued.

There were also some owners who purposely left their pets behind. Dogs were left chained to fences and poles in rising waters. Cats were trapped on roofs of flooded homes. Countless horses and cows were stuck in pens or behind fences. Rescuers and volunteers saved many of these animals, floating them to safety on boats and rafts. Rescuers also swam through floodwaters to untie chains and open gates so penned animals could swim to safety.

Rescued animals were brought to shelters across the state. Many went to Beaumont, Texas. There, two large buildings were turned into animal shelters and filled with cages of lost pets. Volunteers made sure the animals were safe, healthy, and fed. Many owners arrived looking for their animals.

The Beaumont shelter also took in livestock. Volunteers spent days riding horseback in floodwaters to collect loose cattle. Volunteer Amy Walters said, "It's quite the adventure. Alligators were chewing on cows. There's alligators everywhere." Walters wasn't the only person to meet gators in the floodwaters.

Many rescuers carried Hurricane Harvey flood victims so they wouldn't be exposed to harmful chemicals and bacteria in the floodwaters.

CHAPTER 5
DANGEROUS WATERS

When waterways overflow, many wild animals living in them are swept into the floodwaters. These animals can be hard to see. This is because the water stirs up and collects soil and debris, becoming dark and muddy. Alligators and snakes are just some of the dangerous species found in floodwaters. But wild animals weren't the only dangers Harvey's floodwaters held.

CHEMICAL, GARBAGE, AND SEWAGE STEW

Many substances contaminated Harvey's floodwaters, including human and animal waste and spoiled foods. These caused harmful bacteria to grow in the water. Dangerous chemicals from broken containers of cleaning products were swept into Harvey's floodwaters too. So were chemicals from factories, oil refineries, and other businesses.

Harvey floodwaters became a stew of chemicals and disease-causing bacteria, so officials told people to avoid contact with it. However, for thousands of people, this wasn't possible. Many had to wade and swim to safety. Those who did were told to shower immediately after touching the water. But many shelters and homes did not have clean water for showers.

Debris also made traveling in the floodwaters dangerous. Cars, furniture, building materials, and garbage floated everywhere. Some objects had sharp edges or nails sticking out of them. Bumping into these objects was a constant risk.

After days of dealing with contaminated floodwaters, Harris County finally experienced a bit of relief. Harvey moved away, toward Louisiana. The rain stopped and water levels slowly fell. But as floodwaters began to drain, new problems arose.

Edward Woods of Spring, Texas, is one of thousands of residents having to deal with mold. It can be very difficult to remove. In many cases, walls, carpeting, cabinets, and flooring must be replaced.

CHAPTER 6

EVERLASTING AFTERMATH

As Harvey moved away from Harris County, the floodwaters slowly started to drain. Much of the water flowed toward the Gulf of Mexico. Some drained into soil, but much of the soil in the area contains clay, which is poor at absorbing water. And because so much of the Houston area is paved, there was little exposed soil to soak up the water. Harvey's floodwaters took weeks to fully drain.

When the water did finally disappear, new problems became evident. About 156,000 homes in Harris County had flood damage. People returned to their homes to find their belongings wet, stained, and ruined. Floodwaters destroyed appliances. It weakened flooring and walls. Thousands of homes were beyond repair. Others appeared to be habitable but held microscopic dangers.

Mold can spread quickly throughout the interior of a flood-damaged car.

STUBBORN, SICKENING MOLD

Flooded houses and buildings are perfect places for mold to grow. In areas affected by flooding, mold can begin to form within one or two days. It grows on walls, ceilings, and other surfaces.

Once mold starts growing, it spreads quickly by giving off spores. Spores are tiny cells the mold releases into the air.

The spores reproduce to make more mold. They are also invisible to the human eye. People inhale spores without realizing it. Many people are allergic to these spores, and breathing them in causes health issues. Mold also affects people who have breathing conditions such as asthma, causing reactions such as asthma attacks and sore throats. Mold spores can also cause life-threatening lung infections.

Health officials warned Harvey flood victims to clean up any mold in their homes. Homeowners needed to remove waterlogged surfaces where mold had formed, including walls, ceilings, roofs, and carpeting. But this was not possible for all victims.

Tearing down and rebuilding was expensive. So was replacing carpet and furniture. Some people could not afford to rebuild and replace everything that was contaminated by mold. And many of these people could not afford to move somewhere else. *The Atlantic* journalist James Hamblin predicted the lasting effects mold would have on storm victims. He said, "Mold will mark the divide between people who can afford to escape it and people for whom the storm doesn't end."

Many homes were destroyed in Florida during Hurricane Irma. Roofs and walls were torn off. Some homes completely collapsed.

MORE STORMS

As southeastern US states dealt with Harvey's aftermath, another hurricane formed. It was Hurricane Irma. Irma struck Cuba as a Category 5 hurricane on September 9. The next day it became a Category 4 storm before hitting the Florida Keys. A storm surge brought flooding and winds ripped homes apart. Twenty-seven people died. The next week, Hurricane Maria formed in the Atlantic Ocean. Maria struck the US territory of Puerto Rico on September 20. Its winds crushed homes and buildings and toppled power lines.

Back-to-back storms during hurricane season is not unusual, but scientists say Harvey, Irma, and Maria were notable for other reasons. Harvey broke the record for the most rain produced by any tropical cyclone in the continental United States. Irma was unique because of its lasting strength. For thirty-seven hours, its winds blew at 180 miles (290 km) per hour. This was longer than any other storm ever recorded at this speed. Maria damaged or destroyed most of the buildings in Puerto Rico. The country's more than three million residents were left without power, drinking water, and adequate food for weeks.

The United States had never been hit by three hurricanes this strong during the same season. But scientists believe it could happen again. Climate change is causing sea levels and ocean temperatures to rise. These changes do not cause hurricanes. But they can cause hurricanes to be stronger. US meteorologist Sean Sublette said, "As we go forward in time, there's going to be a tendency for the hurricanes that do form to have heavier rain and, perhaps, stronger winds."

Remaining safe, finding shelter, and cleaning up were on most people's minds after Hurricane Harvey. But scientists hope the hurricane and its aftermath will not be forgotten. They want to learn from the storm. And they hope Hurricane Harvey will be remembered not only for its destruction but for its role in helping people prepare for future storms.

Hurricane Maria damaged 90 percent of homes on the island of the Dominica. Water and electrical systems were also ruined.

WHAT YOU CAN DO

A hurricane is an overwhelming event. It is hard to know what to do or how to help others. Here are some things you can do to stay safe during a hurricane, help afterward, and prepare for future storms.

Staying Safe during a Hurricane

- **Listen to officials.** Follow the directions of local leaders. Leave the area if ordered to.
- **Stay inside during landfall.** Remain inside as the storm passes through your area. But stay out of basements and away from windows and doorways.
- **Keep in touch with family and friends.** Call, text, email, or use social media to let friends and family know you are safe or to ask for help if you need it.
- **Check for updates often.** If possible, check for the latest news about the hurricane. Check weather reports on the radio, television, or internet. Follow any new instructions from officials.

Helping after a Hurricane

- **Donate money or goods.** But do some research first. Make sure the charity you donate to has a history of actually giving the donations to victims. Visit Charity Navigator at www.charitynavigator.org to find out more.

STAR POWER

Following Hurricanes Harvey and Irma, many celebrities came together to raise money for victims. On September 12, 2017, famous musicians, actors, and athletes hosted a telethon. Attendees included Beyoncé, Justin Bieber, Leonardo DiCaprio, and more. These stars raised $44 million for hurricane victims!

- **Volunteer.** Do you live near an area affected by a hurricane? Research online to find local organizations accepting volunteers. Volunteer work could include preparing care packages, taking care of lost pets, and more.
- **Adopt or foster a pet.** Thousands of pets become lost during a hurricane. Many end up in animal shelters across the country. Contact a local animal shelter or humane society to see how you can help.

Preparing for Future Hurricanes

- **Make a plan with your family.** Know where to go, who to contact, and what to do if a hurricane hits. Be sure to include a plan to keep your pets safe too.

- **Create a Hurricane supply kit.** Put together a bag or box of items that would be useful during a hurricane. This includes a flashlight and batteries, a first-aid kit, cash, water, and a radio. Lists of important local phone numbers, such as hospitals and the police, are helpful too.

- **Sign up for community text or email alerts.** Many cities, counties, and states offer digital alerts and updates about emergencies and natural disasters.

Many shelters around Texas received donations of clothing, diapers, cleaning supplies, water, food, and more.

HISTORIC HURRICANES

Hurricane Harvey was unforgettable. But the United States has experienced other memorable hurricanes throughout history.

Galveston Hurricane

Galveston Hurricane

Galveston, Texas, September 8, 1900

The Galveston Hurricane remains the deadliest natural disaster in US history. It was a Category 4 storm. Its winds blew at 135 miles (217 km) per hour. Historians are unsure how many people died in the hurricane. But they estimate between six thousand and twelve thousand people died.

Labor Day Hurricane

Florida Keys, September 2, 1935

The Labor Day Hurricane was one of three Category 5 hurricanes to ever hit the United States. It tore across the Upper Keys at more than 200 miles (322 km) per hour. Winds created a large storm surge. It pushed 15 feet (4.6 m) of water onto the islands. A total of 408 people died in the storm.

Hurricane Andrew

Hurricane Andrew

South Florida, August 24, 1992

Hurricane Andrew was also one of the three Category 5 hurricanes to ever hit the United States. Its winds blew at 175 miles (282 km) per hour. The hurricane killed twenty-six people directly. Another thirty-nine people died later from hurricane-related injuries or disease. Andrew also tore through the Miami Metro Zoo. It ruined zoo exhibits and freed animals. Monkeys, wild birds, exotic snakes, and other animals escaped.

Hurricane Katrina

US Gulf Coast, August 29, 2005

Hurricane Katrina was deadly. Its winds reached 140 miles (225 km) per hour. The hurricane was 400 miles (644 km) wide. The storm caused destruction across 90,000 square miles (233,099 sq km) of the United States. Nearly two thousand people died. The worst of the damage was in New Orleans, Louisiana. The city experienced major flooding. Area survivors who were poor struggled to find food, shelter, and work after Katrina. Many feel the US government did not do enough to help these people.

Hurricane Maria

Puerto Rico, September 20, 2017

Hurricane Maria devastated the US territory of Puerto Rico. The Category 4 storm was the third-strongest storm to ever make landfall in the United States. Its winds blew at 155 miles (249 km) per hour. The wind and the extreme flooding that followed damaged most Puerto Rican buildings. The entire island lost power. Numerous people died and thousands didn't have shelter, food, or clean water.

GLOSSARY

absorb: to take in or swallow up

aftermath: the period of time after a bad and usually destructive event

bayou: a body of water, such as a creek that flows slowly through marshy land

chaos: complete confusion and disorder

climate change: changes in Earth's weather patterns

confirm: to make sure that something has definitely happened or is going to happen

contaminate: to make something dangerous, dirty, or impure by adding something harmful or undesirable to it

debris: fragments of wreckage scattered around after a disaster

displace: to force people or animals to leave the area where they live

evacuate: to leave a dangerous area and go somewhere safe

eyewall: a bank of swirling clouds that surrounds the center of a hurricane

habitable: suitable or fit to live in

hurtle: to move or fall with great speed and force

infection: a disease caused by bacteria that enter the body

intense: very strong or great in degree

landfall: when something at sea, such as a storm or boat, reaches shore

meteorologist: a scientist who studies the weather

microscopic: so small it can only be seen through a microscope

overwhelm: to cause someone to have too many things to deal with

prone: likely to do, have, or suffer from something

storm surge: a rise in sea level caused by a hurricane's wind pushing ocean water toward the shore

topple: to fall over

tornado: a rapidly spinning column of air that extends from the base of a thunderstorm to the ground

tributary: a stream flowing into a larger stream or a lake

unique: very special or unusual

SOURCE NOTES

9   Jason Samenow, "The Forgotten but Freakish Damage from Hurricane Harvey's Eyewall in Rockport, Tex.," *Washington Post*, September 1, 2017, https://www.washingtonpost.com/news/capital-weather-gang/wp/2017/09/01/the-forgotten-but-freakish-damage-from-hurricane-harveys-eyewall-in-rockport-tex/?utm_term=.f440a87c5a3d

10   Kevin Sullivan, Tim Craig, and Joel Achenbach, "Harvey Delivers Heavy Damage as It Batters Texas Coast," *Washington Post*, August 26, 2017, https://www.washingtonpost.com/national/hurricane-harvey-hits-texas-bringing-high-winds-storm-surge/2017/08/26/64fa6982-8a28-11e7-a50f-e0d4e6ec070a_story.html?utm_term=.214846270bd2

19   Brian Mann, "From Pets to Livestock, Lost Animals Rounded Up in Beaumont's Makeshift Shelter," *All Things Considered*, NPR, September 4, 2017, http://www.npr.org/2017/09/04/548433503/from-pets-to-livestock-lost-animals-rounded-up-in-beaumont-s-makeshift-shelter

24   James Hamblin, "The Looming Consequences of Breathing Mold," *Atlantic*, August 30, 2017, https://www.theatlantic.com/health/archive/2017/08/mold-city/538224/

25   Wayne Drash, "Yes, Climate Change Made Harvey and Irma Worse," CNN, September 19, 2017, http://www.cnn.com/2017/09/15/us/climate-change-hurricanes-harvey-and-irma/index.html

FURTHER READING AND WEBSITES

Challoner, Jack. *Eyewitness Hurricane & Tornado*. New York: DK Publishing, 2014.

FEMA, Collection: Hurricane Safety Graphics
    https://www.fema.gov/pt-br/media-library/multimedia/collections/506

Kostigen, Thomas. *Extreme Weather: Surviving Tornadoes, Sandstorms, Hailstorms, Blizzards, Hurricanes, and More!* Washington, DC: National Geographic, 2014.

Mooney, Carla. *Surviving in Wild Waters*. Minneapolis: Lerner Publications, 2013.

National Geographic Kids: Hurricane
    http://kids.nationalgeographic.com/explore/science/hurricane/#hurricane-aletta.jpg

Owings, Lisa. *What Protects Us during Natural Disasters?* Minneapolis: Lerner Publications, 2016.

Pratt, Mary K. *Hurricane Katrina and the Flooding of New Orleans: A Cause-and-Effect Investigation.* Minneapolis: Lerner Publications, 2017.

Ready.gov: Floods
    https://www.ready.gov/kids/know-the-facts/floods

Zullo, Allan. *Heroes of Hurricane Katrina*. New York: Scholastic Inc., 2015.

INDEX

PHOTO ACKNOWLEDGMENTS

The images in this book are used with the permission of: ©Lost & Taken, all backgrounds; ©NASA Earth Observatory image by Jesse Allen, using data from the Land Atmosphere Near real-time Capability for EOS (LANCE). Caption by Adam Voiland., p. 4; ©Eric V Overton/Shutterstock, pp. 6, 23; ©zstock/Shutterstock, p. 7; ©AMFPhotography/Shutterstock, p. 8; ©Nick Wagner/Austin American-Statesman via AP, p. 9; ©brichuas/Shutterstock, p. 10; ©AP Photo/Eric Gay, p. 11; ©MDay Photography/Shutterstock, p. 12; ©Elizabeth Conley/Houston Chronicle via AP, p. 13; ©Karl Spencer/ iStockphoto, p. 14; US Department of Defense, pp. 15, 16; Texas National Guard/Flickr, p. 17; US Department of Defense/ Flickr, p. 18; Air Force Magazine/Flickr, p. 19; US Customs and Border Protection/Flickr, p. 20; ©AP Photo/David J. Phillip, p. 22; ©Jodi Jacobson/iStockphoto, p. 24; ©JEAN-FRANCOIS Manuel/Shutterstock, p. 25; ©All Stock Photos/ Shutterstock, p. 27; Library of Congress, p. 28 (top); ©Joseph Sohm/Shutterstock, p. 28 (bottom); ©imaginewithme/ iStockphoto, p. 29. Cover photographs ©AP Photo/David J. Phillip (front); ©Eric V Overton/Shutterstock (back); ©Lost & Taken (background).